IMAGES OF
WEST CORNWALL

Simon Cook

HALSGROVE

First published in Great Britain in 2002

Title page photograph: Porthmeor

British Library Cataloguing-in-Publication Data
A CIP record for this title is available from the British Library

ISBN 1 84114 206 9

HALSGROVE
PUBLISHING, MEDIA AND DISTRIBUTION

Halsgrove House
Lower Moor Way
Tiverton, Devon EX16 6SS
Tel: 01884 243242
Fax: 01884 243325
email sales@halsgrove.com
website www.halsgrove.com

Printed in Italy by Centro Grafico Ambrosiano, Milan

INTRODUCTION

Born in 1960 at Ding Dong in Penwith, I grew up oblivious to my surroundings. As a child the moors around the family house were taken for granted, one huge playground. A place in which to build camps, an area in which to adventure, to climb the granite tors or shimmy down the shallow mine workings hidden amongst the bracken and occasionally feel the fear of unknown depths echoed up from a tossed stone clattering down the not so shallow mine shafts!

Blind to the everyday landscape around me I moved to London in my early twenties, returning twelve years later, a father, a photographer and perhaps a more insightful man. I returned with the knowledge that Penwith is a gem, not one of a dozen places to be found anywhere. The man-made landscape of the cities can offer much within its urban environment. But Penwith, meaning 'the far end', surrounded by the sea on three sides offers a unique peninsular, an open space in which to feel the wonder of nature, the timelessness of the sun, wind and rain and see the natural art and sculpture carved into the granite surroundings.

This series of images came from an initial idea of providing a weekly landscape feature for the local paper *The Cornishman* in 1995. The purpose of the views for me were to remind readers of places they may not have visited before or a favourite area not seen for a while. To encourage people to go out and enjoy Penwith, something it is easy to neglect when living and working in the district, but the reason why many people have moved to Cornwall in the first place. I wanted to bring back a memory to the older inhabitants who perhaps can no longer climb and hike as they once could in younger days and to remind those who have moved away, gone abroad or are visiting, of the inherent beauty of this area. *Images of West Cornwall* brings together the best of these. Whether a visitor or local, enjoy this photographic tour.

Simon Cook

Down off his Ding Dong downs
with his buzzard-eyed view
to frame and capture and celebrate
those carns, zawns and nans
those porths and downs
A Cornishman breath of fresh air

By Kurt Jackson

Ding Dong Mine

SPRING

Bishops Head and Foot

Boskennal Mill

Lower Bossow

Bosullow Common

The Crowns

Wheal Edwards Tin Mine

Horses grazing, Botallack

Carn Galva Tin Mine

Across Porthmeor Farm to Carn Galva

Carnyorth, Pendeen

Cotton-like flowers of moorland grasses in full bloom on Chykembro Common, Newmill

Chywoone Grove

Lamorna from the coast path

Buttercups adorn Madron Carn

Bluebells at Madron Carn

St Michael's Mount seen from Maen-Du Point

Men Scryfa marks the spot where Ryalvran, 'the Royal Raven', was killed in battle in the 5th or 6th century

St Michael's Mount, Mounts Bay.

Boat repairs, Mousehole

Mousehole Harbour

Newmill Village

The view from Tredinneck looking South East across Newmill

Mulfra Quoit with Tredinneck and Green Burrow (on skyline) engine houses behind

Old Carn looking towards Trencrom

Porthmeor Farm, Treen

Retallack Ponds

Prussia Cove

Prussia Cove

The River Hayle, St Erth

Across St Ives from Rosewall Hill

St Ives

Coastal path, St Loy

Tredavoe Methodist Chapel

Tregadgwith

Tregurtha Downs

Trengwainton Gardens

Trevaylor Woods

Trevean Cliff

Trewellard Bottoms

Foxgloves, Zennor

Zennor

SUMMER

Boarding for St Michael's Mount

Decommissioned Fishing Boats being broken up in Newlyn Harbour

Cape Cornwall with the Brisons beyond

Carn Barges, Sennen. (One of at least three places called 'Carn Barges' within Penwith)

The South coast from Carn Barges to Carn Scathe

Tater-du from Carn Barges

Carn Boel and the Longships light house

Carnaquidden, New Mill

Cudden Point

Godrevy Sands

Gulval Church

Sunflowers, Gulval

Hayle Bar

Hayle Bar ten minutes later

In Mounts Bay

Jubilee pool, Penzance

Lamorna Cove

Men-an-Tol

Nancledra

Newbridge

Newlyn Harbour

Newlyn

Nancledra

Porthgwarra

Porth Chapple

Porth Kidney

The 1798 folly 'Rogers Tower'

Aerial View looking across Sancreed towards the North Coast

St Ives Harbour

Pig Huts, St Just

Coastal path, St Loy

Woodland near Trewoofe, Lamorna

Trowan Cliff near St Ives

AUTUMN

Beagletodn Downs, Towednack

Across Boswens Common to Bosullow

Sunset at Carn Galva mine

Cot Valley

Gurnards Head

Knill Monument built as an intended mausoleum for himself in 1782,
St Ives Mayor John Knill was later buried in London

Higher Ninnis

Lands End

Early Morning, Lanyon Quoit

Morvah

Pontshallow

Across the estuary to the Riviere Towans

Rosemergy

The Roundhouse, Sennen

Sunset from the North Road, Pendeen

Sunset at Lands End

Trendrine

Trevaylor Woods

Trevowhan Cliff

Watch Croft, Morvah

Zennor Quoit

WINTER

Barnoon Cemetry, St Ives

Beersheba

Bodrifty Iron Age Village, Newmill

Standing stone, Boskednan

Across Bossow to Halestown

Cape Cornwall

Carn Galva mine

Carn Gloose to Gurnards Head

The Iron Age stone works of Chun Castle

Chun Hill

Chun Quoit

Chypraze Cliff

Looking North East from Carn Galva across Porthmeor towards Zennor

Rosemergy from Carn Galva

Georgia Mine

Godrevy light house

Green Burrow tin mine

Gwynver Beach

Hayle

Kenidjack, St Just

Little Galva

Bait Digging, Long Rock

Gig launches into the bay at Long Rock

Madron

The Causeway at low tide, Marazion

Marazion seen from St Michael's Mount

White Downs

Penberth

Rain with sunny patches on the road to Pendeen Watch

Porthmeor Beach, St Ives

Portheras Cove

Portheras Cove

Rosemodress Cliff

Winter skies send shafts of sunlight over Carn Galva

The Towans, Hayle

Church of St Tewennocus, Towednack

Treen Cove, Gurnards Head

Trencrom Hill

Trevarnon Farm

Tredinneck

The view across Trevethoe Barton to the misty heights of Trencrom Hill